Steam Around
The Hampshire
& Dorset Coast

Mike Arlett & David Lockett

Ian Allan
PUBLISHING

Right: High Noon at Southampton Central! With the station clock showing mid-day, the fireman of 'Battle of Britain' class 4-6-2 No 34072 *257 Squadron* takes the opportunity to pull forward some coal whilst water is taken before restarting a train bound for Portsmouth. This is one of the unmodified Bulleid light Pacifics which can still be seen, having been restored to full working order and re-steamed in 1990 for the first time since 1964 (the same year that Norman Lockett took this picture). Based on the Swanage Railway, one of the lines featured within this album, No 34072 has spent a busy decade in service on the Purbeck Line.

All photographs in this book by Norman Lockett, copyright David Lockett

Introduction

David Lockett has explained to me that, when it came to railway enthusiasm, his father was, first and foremost, very much a Great Western man. It therefore came as some surprise to see just how much Norman Lockett photographed, in colour, the Southern Region from the late 1950s until the demise of Southern steam in July 1967! However, colour photography, certainly in the late 1950s, was considered by Norman Lockett (and indeed by some other leading exponents of railway photography of that same era) as 'experimental' or, as Norman wrote in one of his notebooks, 'not to be taken seriously'! Thank goodness, during that period, some persevered with this medium; none more so than Dick (R. C.) Riley and Peter Gray, and a few others whose splendid efforts preceded the start of the 1960s, which proved to be the 'threshold' after which colour film gained rapidly in popularity amongst railway photographers.

Norman Lockett's colour transparencies featuring Southern Region steam range far and wide, but this book concentrates mostly on a number of lines (both major and minor) which led to the sea or, in some cases, were surrounded by it! It covers an area from Hayling Island, on the South Coast, westwards through Southampton and Bournemouth to Weymouth. On the way, we have taken in brief diversions to a southern remnant of the Meon Valley line, the motive power depot and 'scrap lines' at Eastleigh, and a trip across the Solent to visit the Isle of Wight. Further westwards, the locations visited include the Lymington and Swanage branch lines whilst, at Weymouth, no visit would be complete without a quick foray along that unique stretch of rails leading to the quay (albeit that the motive power was still ex-Great Western!). We finish with just one view of the line to Portland. So, in effect, this album starts with an 'island' (at Hayling), visits a real one (the Isle of Wight) and a near-one (the 'Isle' of Purbeck) and concludes with another, at Portland!

With the approval of our publisher, David Lockett and I have given deliberate emphasis to those branch lines which Norman visited on a number of occasions. Thus the Havant to Hayling Island and the Isle of Wight (featuring all but exclusively the section between Ryde Pier Head and Smallbrook Junction) are given due prominence in the knowledge that none of the colour pictures illustrating these lines has previously appeared within the covers of a book. Indeed, we are confident that very nearly all of the pictures contained in the following pages have never previously been published.

We have also tried to balance the number of pictures between Bulleid Pacifics and other classes of motive power! So many books which feature former Southern Region steam appear to consist of page after page of these (splendid) locomotives. Even so, by the early 1960s, it was becoming ever more difficult to photograph anything else, particularly on the main lines of the 'Southern'! Of course, if one travelled the Hayling branch, one could photograph nothing other than the delightful little 'A1X' class 0-6-0s, whilst, on the Isle of Wight, by this period, it was 'Class O2 0-4-4Ts or nothing'. So we have to advise you in advance that these two classes feature prominently in this book!

Little attempt has been made to provide detailed histories of the lines or, in most cases, the locomotives featured in the following pages; these subjects have already been covered in other publications. This book is intended to portray, in colour, what (with but a few notable exceptions) were once everyday scenes; perhaps many were so 'everyday' that we took them far too much for granted. Only, as a railway enthusiast, if you can recall that era are you able to understand fully the excitement of a holiday which started and ended by steam train — an event which, at that time, seemed like a major adventure into the unknown but which, today, would be seen as no

First published 2001

ISBN 0 7110 2794 3

© Mike Arlett & David Lockett 2001

Published by Ian Allan Publishing

an imprint of Ian Allan Publishing Ltd, Hersham, Surrey KT12 4RG.
Printed by Ian Allan Printing Ltd, Hersham, Surrey KT12 4RG.

Code: 0105/B2

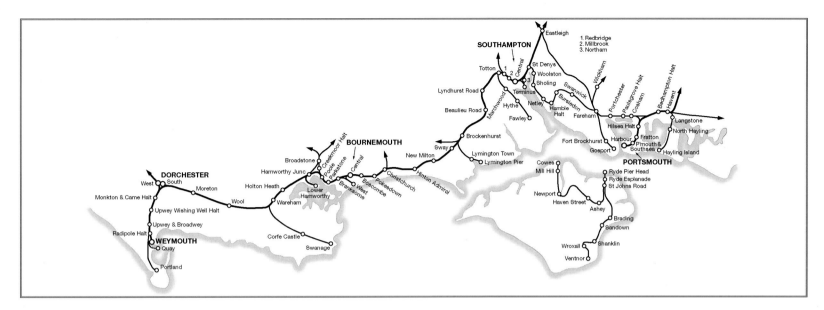

more than 'a trip down the road'! Any and every excursion to a destination, however close or far but which happened to lie within a different Region of British Railways, was exciting because of the 'foreign' motive power and the differences in railway infrastructure and atmosphere. The younger railway enthusiasts of the 1950s (that golden postwar era of the 'trainspotter'), many requiring no more for a day's entertainment than an Ian Allan *abc*, a penny platform ticket and a bottle of 'Tizer', were, I feel, a very different breed from those who followed later and helped spawn the legend of the railway 'anorak'. Most from that earlier era grew up to appreciate that there was much more of interest to railways than taking locomotive numbers. Sadly, however, it was all but too late: steam was on the way out, Dr Beeching was on the way in, and branch and cross-country railway lines everywhere were under increasing threat of closure.

Hopefully, this book will evoke more than a few happy memories for those who can still recall at least some of the locations featured in its pages. Many of the lines included still exist, of course, but when one compares what is left today with the system of but 35 to 40 years ago, one realises just how much has been lost. Thankfully, sections of two of the branch lines featured are the subject of successful and still-developing restoration schemes. The Isle of Wight Steam Railway, with its unique collection of coaching stock may, one day, again reach Ryde or, perhaps, even the outskirts of Newport (or both!). In these days of Heritage Lottery funding, schemes which just a few years ago seemed but 'pipe dreams' may now be just possible. The other restored line is, of course, the Swanage Railway — a marvellous line which, under a sound management, is working towards the objective of restoring a link with the main-line system. Indeed, even as this introduction is penned (or word-processed!), the gap between the Swanage Railway and the Railtrack railhead at Furzebrook grows ever smaller. So here, as at the sites of other preservation schemes (not least the Mid-Hants, the Bluebell and the Kent & East Sussex railways, all of which lie outside the area covered by this book), it is still possible for today's generation to savour, in a small way, something of what Southern steam was all about! Long may they all prosper.

Mike Arlett
North Bradley, Wiltshire
Spring 2001

Havant, to the east of Portsmouth, is the junction for the main lines to London and Brighton. Until late 1963, this was also the junction for the 4½-mile branch line to Hayling Island, and it was this little line which Norman Lockett visited to photograph in 1959 and, again, in 1963 — the last summer before closure of the branch. The main attraction, of course, was the motive power, the services hauled by the little 'Terrier' class locomotives. By the early 1960s these were the oldest locomotives still at work on British Railways. Here, No 32650, resplendent in BR lined black livery, is about to set off for Hayling from the bay platform at Havant. Just visible in the background is another 'Terrier' which had brought in the previous service.

No 32661, dwarfed by its two coaches, sets off from Havant, the branch line commencing with a curve which soon sharpened to carry the rails southwards through a 90° turn. Designed by William Stroudley for the London, Brighton & South Coast Railway (LBSCR), a total of 50 of the 'Terrier' 0-6-0T locomotives were built between 1872 and 1880. Some were scrapped or sold off as long ago as 1899. Of the remainder, from 1911 these were rebuilt as Class A1X. By the mid-1950s 12 still remained, of which no fewer than 10 survived into preservation. No 32661 was not among these survivors.

Left: As a thunderstorm threatens, No 32646 hurries around the reverse curves southeast of Havant. Perhaps in the knowledge that this was likely to prove the final summer of service, somebody has taken a paintbrush and 'livened up' the front end of No 32646 including the smokebox door hinges and numberplate! 'No 46' led a varied life. Built in 1876, it spent time on the Lyme Regis branch and on the Freshwater, Yarmouth & Newport Railway. The locomotive was retained on the Isle of Wight until 1949, after which it was a regular performer on the Hayling line. Following withdrawal in late 1963, it was purchased for preservation but sold on into the ownership of a brewery which displayed the locomotive outside the 'Hayling Billy' public house. In 1979, the brewery gave the locomotive to the Wight Locomotive Society, which restored it to traffic on the Isle of Wight Steam Railway as No 8 *Freshwater* — a name carried during some of its years previously spent on the island.

Right: The reason for the continued retention of the diminutive 'Terriers', which weighed in at just 28 tons 5cwt, was the severe weight restriction on the 1,000ft-long bridge which carried the line across Langstone Harbour. Nothing heavier was permitted across this wooden structure, the condition and cost of upgrading of which were primary factors in the closure of the branch line. The bridge was also the reason all the 'Terriers' working on the branch were fitted with spark-arresters! No 32650 approaches the northern end of the bridge and regains the 'mainland' on a return run from Hayling to Havant. Note the modern leading carriage, No S1000S, a one-off experimental design constructed with an all-plastic body and three differing internal decors.

Above: Unfortunately, we have found only a single picture taken by Norman Lockett which 'features' the terminus station at Hayling Island. It is really more a portrait of a 'Terrier', with No 32650 standing by the coal stage. Only the lupins, by the station nameboard, provide a small splash of colour to this scene. No 32650 was another of the 'A1X' class to survive into preservation.

Right: Norman Lockett's superb study of Langstone Bridge, as photographed from the parallel road bridge, shows just how diminutive the Class A1X 0-6-0T 'Terriers' were in comparison with the coaching stock, which again includes the experimental all-plastic coach, itself of a lower profile than the two following vehicles. The locomotive, drifting across the bridge (to minimise stress), is about to cross the swing-bridge section which could be opened manually under the control of the signalbox seen perched on the side of the bridge.

Below: South of Langstone station, No 32646 heads towards Langstone Bridge during the final year of services. The Havant–Hayling Island train is just passing over the points of the long-disused siding which once served a wharf adjacent to the Hayling road bridge.

Right: On the approach to Havant, No 32650 is again captured on film by Norman Lockett, here in the early-evening sunshine, nearing the end of the return run from Hayling Island. Built as No 50 *Whitechapel* by the LBSCR in 1876, and following service on the Isle of Wight and at Lancing, No 32650 was destined to work the last public passenger train from Hayling Island on 3 November 1963. Subsequently, the locomotive was purchased as a proposed public exhibit in the London Borough of Sutton but was placed with the Kent & East Sussex Railway, which has since maintained the 'Terrier' under the guise of No 10 (or 32650) *Sutton.*

Left: At the end of the run, No 32640 takes on water at the buffer stops serving the bay platform at Havant. This was the only watering point available on the branch. Smokebox ash can be seen piled against the concrete post and panel fencing which, like the platform edge supports, were the products of the Southern Railway concrete works located at Exmouth Junction, Exeter. No 32640 had been built in 1878 as No 40 *Brighton*, and was sent by the LBSCR to the Paris Exhibition, gaining a gold medal. In 1902 it was sold to the Isle of Wight Central Railway, where it became No 11 and was later given the name *Newport*. It returned to the mainland in 1947, and the following year, upon nationalisation of the railways, regained its original number with the addition of 32600! Withdrawn in December 1963, the locomotive was restored externally for sale to Butlin's for display at the holiday camp at Pwllheli. It later returned to the Isle of Wight where, following superb restoration to full working order, it now runs again as No 11 *Newport*.

Above: Before leaving Havant, just one more of the many Norman Lockett transparencies featuring the Hayling 'Terriers'. No 32650, fitted with a Drummond-style chimney, pauses alongside No 32640 which still retained the original and more elegant Stroudley chimney.

About 12 miles to the west of Havant, Fareham is reached. From here, the line to Alton — the Meon Valley line — which had once served as part of a through route from Waterloo to Gosport and Stokes Bay, was closed to regular passenger traffic in early February 1955. At the same time, the central part of this branch line, between Farringdon and Droxford, closed completely. Six years later, on 30 April 1961, the Locomotive Club of Great Britain (LCGB) ran a special train, the 'Solent Limited', which included a run up the remaining southern section of the line from Fareham to Droxford. Here, the special pulls away from Wickham, hauled by Class E1 0-6-0T No 32694 and Class O2 0-4-4T No 30200. The tour proved to be one of the final duties of No 32694, the sole surviving 'E1', which was withdrawn in the summer of 1961.

Right: Class T9 4-4-0 No 30117 had brought the 'Solent Limited' to Fareham. Whilst the special visited the remnants of Meon Valley line and then traversed the branch to Gosport and back, the 'T9' rested at Fareham, waiting to take over again for the next leg of the journey. By this date, only a few of the famous Drummond 'Greyhounds', first introduced in 1899, remained in service. No 30117 had been selected as the example to be retained for preservation, but in the event this choice was subsequently amended, and No 30120 was saved instead. No 30117 was withdrawn in July 1961.

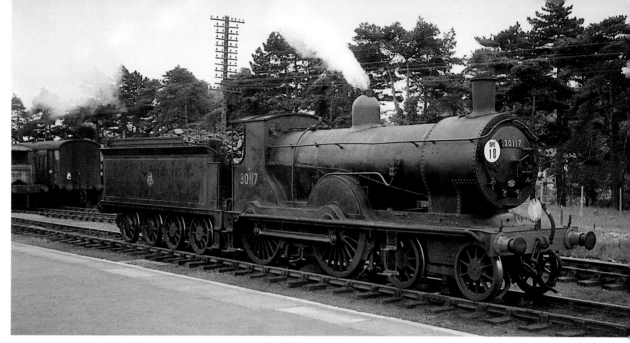

Left: Class E1 0-6-0T No 32694 and Class O2 0-4-4T No 30200 arrive back at Fareham, having completed the return trip along the Gosport branch which, since the cessation of passenger trains in June 1953, had remained open for freight traffic. The 'T9' 4-4-0, No 30117, waits for the two tank engines to be uncoupled, run clear and hand over the special for the next leg of the railtour.

Above: Fareham remains the junction for the coastal line to Southampton and for the route to Eastleigh, our next port of call, which Norman Lockett photographed in colour during visits made in the late 1950s and early 1960s. Here, in addition to the Works, there was a large motive power depot. This line-up of engines is outside the eastern end of the shed and includes ex-LBSCR 0-6-0T Stroudley 'Terrier' No 32646, a pair of ex-LSWR Drummond Class M7 0-4-4Ts — of which No 30328 is the nearer — and an example of somewhat more modern motive power in the form of BR Standard Class 4 4-6-0 No 75066. The difference in the ages of the 'Terrier' and the BR 'Standard' is 78 years!

Above right: No 30506, one of the original Urie Class S15 4-6-0s designed for express freight traffic and built at Eastleigh in 1920. The design was later developed by Maunsell, who built further examples, and could be seen on both passenger and freight duties. Withdrawn in 1964, No 30506 was later purchased from Barry Scrapyard and, following restoration, was based at the Mid-Hants Railway, where the locomotive can still be seen.

Right: Class D1 4-4-0 No 31735, a Maunsell rebuild (dating from 1921) of the former SECR Class D introduced by Wainwright in 1901. The rebuilding of 21 of the class altered quite dramatically the appearance of these locomotives, compared with those remaining in original condition.

Below: A famous old lady awaits her fate! No 30584, one of the Class 0314 4-4-2 Adams radial tanks, was withdrawn in February 1961, following many years of service on the Lyme Regis branch. In weather conditions which reflect this sad scene, No 30584 awaits cutting-up. The builder's plate, showing the locomotive to have been built by Dübs & Co in 1885, had already been removed from the splasher of the leading driving wheel. This engine first entered service as LSWR No 520.

Right: An even older locomotive: No 30585, one of the Class 0298 2-4-0 Beattie well tanks dating from 1874, although rebuilt at Eastleigh in 1921. Originally a large number of these locomotives had been constructed, but by as early as 1898 all bar three had been withdrawn. The trio of survivors was destined to last another 64 years, retained for working the line to Wenford Bridge in Cornwall. Two of these locomotives escaped the cutter's torch, including No 30585 which is now based at the Buckinghamshire Railway Centre, Quainton, near Aylesbury. Standing behind the well tank, Drummond Class T9 4-4-0 'Greyhound' No 30287 waits to be cut up.

Below: To the Isle of Wight... Stationed at their pontoon in Portsmouth Harbour, PS *Ryde* (left), built in 1937, and PS *Sandown* dating from 1934, were the last two paddle-steamers ordered by the Southern Railway for the Isle of Wight services. Both were built by William Denny & Bros Ltd of Dumbarton. *Sandown* was withdrawn at the end of the 1965 summer season and was scrapped; *Ryde* remained in service until 1969. The latter was subsequently moved to a berth at Binfield Marina, upstream from Cowes on the River Medina, where, renamed *Ryde Queen*, she was used as a clubhouse and discotheque. Despite being damaged by fire in 1977, the old paddle-steamer was soon renovated but later fell into disrepair, and is still awaiting a restoration scheme.

Right: Ryde Pier Head station, as seen from the same viewpoint as the picture on the front cover of this book but, on this occasion, with the sun proving less co-operative! Class O2 0-4-4T No 26 *Whitwell* pulls away from Platform 2 with a train for Cowes. There are, in fact, three piers here: the structure used by the railway and opened in 1880; the second (seen in the foreground) dating from 1864 and used, until closure in late-January 1969, by the trams which shuttled to and fro along the pier; and the third — the Promenade Pier — from which Norman Lockett obtained this picture.

Left: No 35 *Freshwater* has run the length of the pier at Ryde to arrive at Esplanade station. The crossover between the two running lines was retained for emergency use only, and released by an Annett's key under the control of the signalman in the Pier Head signalbox, which can just be seen towards the far end of the pier. On such a beautiful day, the coastline of the mainland is clearly visible across Spithead; the three piers can be seen more clearly in this view. The superstructure carrying the railway was much rebuilt during the winters of 1963/4 and 1966/7. Whilst both tracks still remain, today only the up line is in use between the Esplanade and Pier Head stations. The latter was also rationalised/rebuilt with two platforms instead of four in the mid-1960s.

Above: At the other end of Ryde Esplanade station, No 18 *Ningwood* restarts a train for Cowes, the line descending at 1 in 50 from the station to pass through Ryde Tunnel before reaching St Johns Road station. The line between the Pier Head and St Johns Road stations had been built jointly by the LSWR and LBSCR, and opened from St Johns Road to Esplanade in April 1880 and onwards to Pier Head just three months later. The steamer services from Ryde were also jointly owned prior to the 1923 Grouping of the railways.

Class O2 No 29 *Alverstone* arrives at Ryde St Johns Road station with a
train for Cowes. Located 1½ miles from the Pier Head, this was the location
of the island's railway works, a part of which can be seen in the right
background.

Above: The motive power depot at Ryde was sited on the opposite (up) side of the station, and can be seen in this view behind the large signalbox at St Johns Road. The box, like just about everything used on the island's railway system, was a 'second-hand' transfer from the mainland, in 1928! No 16 *Ventnor* waits to come off shed; the other locomotives in the background feature also in the following picture.

Right: A line-up of Class O2 0-4-4Ts outside the engine shed at Ryde. On the left, No 24 *Calbourne* stands on the coaling road, whilst No 33 *Bembridge* and No 18 *Ningwood* await their next turns of duty. The main point of interest, however, is No 25 *Godshill*, which appears to be in ex-works condition and carries an interesting headcode! The leather case in which Norman Lockett carried his camera for black-and-white photography (still using plate-glass negatives) can be seen on the ground in the right foreground, near the back corner of the signalbox.

A final view of St Johns Road, with No 29 *Alverstone* setting off and passing under the gantry of starting signals. The fact that two of the dolls on the gantry are devoid of signal arms reveals that Norman Lockett took this picture during the summer period when the route from St Johns Road to Smallbrook Junction was being operated as a double-line block section. The red-liveried vehicle on the right is a part of the Works train.

No 17 *Seaview* climbs through a picturesque wooded section between Ryde and Smallbrook Junction with a train for Cowes. Barely visible, against the face of the stone overbridge, is a signal gantry with two dolls, the left carrying the up distant signal for St Johns Road. Out of summer season, this section of track reverted to two single parallel lines — the left with the block section extending from Haven Street (on the Newport line) to St Johns Road, the right from Brading on the Ventnor line. When such arrangements were in operation, a second distant signal was provided on the gantry seen here to serve what became the separate route from Brading. Nearly 40 years later, both sets of rails are still in use on the section of line between Ryde Esplanade and Smallbrook, where an interchange platform now exists for passengers wishing to travel on the Isle of Wight Steam Railway.

Left: No 24 *Calbourne,* with a six-coach train bound for Ventnor, approaches the signalbox at Smallbrook Junction as the fireman prepares to collect the single-line token for the section ahead to Brading. The line serving the route to Newport and Cowes can be seen to the left. *Calbourne* was withdrawn in March 1967 and put aside at Ryde for preservation, and in mid-August 1969 was transferred by road to Newport. Following restoration, it can still be seen on the Isle of Wight Steam Railway, which has its headquarters and workshop at Haven Street station.

Right: Another exchange of a single-line token for the section from Smallbrook to Brading: No 32 *Bonchurch* runs past with a train from Ryde. For the reasons already explained, the signalbox at Smallbrook functioned only during the summer season. At other times this ceased to be a junction, and the signal arms were taken down each autumn.

Left: The signalman in charge of the diminutive signalbox at Smallbrook Junction is handed the token for the single line from Brading as No 30 *Shorwell* passes and is about to regain double track with a train from the Ventnor line.

As mentioned in the Introduction to this book, Norman Lockett's photographic visits to the railways of the Isle of Wight concentrated on the section between Ryde and Smallbrook Junction (understandable when, on summer Saturdays in 1964, it was still possible to see 10 trains an hour on this section!). However, to conclude this brief excursion to 'Vectis' we have included the two following photographs, featuring respectively Shanklin,

Above: When the line from Ryde St Johns was first opened, in 1864, Shanklin was the terminus, the extension to Ventnor not being completed until two years later. Here No 35 *Freshwater* calls with a train from Ryde to await clearance of the single line ahead to Wroxall and Ventnor — a 4-mile journey which included a 1½-mile climb at a gradient of 1 in 70. Notice just how neat and tidy the station was kept. The roof of the signalbox is just visible above the canopy of the up platform on the left. Since 1966 the station has again served as a terminus, but now for the 8½ miles of the third-rail electrified services from Ryde Pier Head; today, only the original single platform remains in use.

Right: Before returning to the mainland, this last photograph from the Isle of Wight features the view from the platform end at Ventnor. Having run round its train, No 20 *Shanklin* eases forward to couple-up for the return run to Ryde. Ventnor Tunnel (1,312yd in length) and signalbox can be seen in the background. The Isle of Wight Railway, having extended from Shanklin, commenced public services to Ventnor on 10 September 1866. This same section closed to traffic on 18 April 1966. The bricked-up tunnel mouth is all that now survives as a reminder of this scene.

Left: Southampton Central: dominated by the 100ft-high clock tower, erected in 1892 but, sadly, demolished late in 1966 prior to the redevelopment of this side of the station which included a five-storey building. Newly fitted with an oblong Giesl ejector (as witnessed in this view by the shape of the chimney), 'Battle of Britain' No 34064 *Fighter Command* draws to a stand at Platform 1 with a Bournemouth West to Waterloo express. Standing at Platform 2, a rebuilt light Pacific rests after arrival with a train from Salisbury.

Above: Another Southampton landmark, the clock tower to the Civic Centre, dominates the skyline as rebuilt 'Battle of Britain' class No 34056 *Croydon* sets off eastwards and towards Southampton Tunnel with a train for Waterloo.

Left: Unlike its competitors, the Southern Railway did not provide water troughs from which locomotives could replenish their tenders whilst on the move. Station waiting time at Southampton was often used, therefore, to take on water. The tender of 'West Country' Pacific No 34023 *Blackmore Vale* is topped up before departing with an express to Waterloo. In the left background, another train sets off westwards from Platform 4.

Above: The classic view at the west end of Southampton Central featuring the impressive signal gantry. This scene featuring the down 'Bournemouth Belle' was selected because of the activity taking place during the scheduled pause at Southampton. As steam blows off skywards from rebuilt 'West Country' No 34047 *Callington*, the fireman tugs on the chain of the water column to swing the 'bag' into position. Farther along the platform, two Pullman-car staff attend to passenger luggage.

Above: From just about the same viewpoint as the previous picture, but now including the large Southampton Central signalbox, which dated from 1935 and remained in use until early November 1981, BR Class 3 2-6-2T No 82014, constructed at Swindon in 1951, drifts through the station with a train of empty oil tanks bound for the refineries at Fawley. Note the obligatory pair of 'barrier wagons' placed between the locomotive and the leading oil tank.

Left: Class V 4-4-0 No 30904 *Lancing* has just backed onto stock in the down bay platform, probably to form a semi-fast service to Bournemouth West. Better remembered as the 'Schools' class, designed by R. E. L. Maunsell and introduced in 1930, many of these famous locomotives were later modified by Bulleid with the fitting of a multiple-jet blastpipe and large-diameter chimney. No 30904, however, remained in original condition.

Earlier (see pages 14 and 15), we featured the LCGB railtour, the 'Solent Limited'. This special also visited the dockside lines at Southampton, although by this stage of the trip the weather had definitely taken a turn for the worse! 'USA' class 0-6-0T No 30073 eases the special across the wet tarmac of Canute Road. The vehicles in the background, including the Ford Anglia, were a common sight in the early 1960s, but today are considered as 'classic' cars.

Another special which utilised an 0-6-0 'USA' tank for part of the itinerary. No 30074 hauls the 'Hampshire Venturer', organised by the Southern Counties Touring Society (SCTS), westwards along the main line at Millbrook on 10 March 1963. The goods yard on the left was closed in 1967 and redeveloped as Southampton's first Freightliner terminal. The iron gates to the right once provided rail access at the western end of Southampton's Western Dock complex.

Having crossed the River Test, Totton station — the junction for the branch line to Fawley — is reached three miles west of Southampton Central. A special, the 'South Western Limited' organised by the LCGB on 18 September 1960, included a run along the branch to Fawley. Class N15 'King Arthur' 4-6-0 No 30782 *Sir Brian* (which had remained at Totton whilst the special visited the branch) waits to set off westwards on the next leg of the journey which travelled, via Brockenhurst and Ringwood, to Broadstone and Hamworthy Junction, the route of the original main line from Southampton to Dorchester.

Above: On an overcast day in 1966, Ivatt Class 2 2-6-2T No 41230 arrives back at Brockenhurst with a branch-line train from Lymington. By this date, the third-rail electrification works for the Bournemouth route were in hand. The conductor rail is already in position on one line whilst, for the nearest track, the supports are in place ready to receive the 'third rail', lengths of which can be seen lying between the running rails.

Right: Four years earlier, in 1962, the local branch-line passenger services were still in the control of the elderly Drummond Class M7 0-4-4 tanks which had been regular performers for many years and would remain as such until 1964. Thereafter, the branch-line services became the domain of the Ivatt 2-6-2Ts and BR 2-6-4Ts. Here, No 30057 runs along the main line, the junction for the 5¾-mile Lymington branch being located about ¾ mile west of Brockenhurst. Lymington Junction was also the location where the direct route to Bournemouth parted company with the original route from Southampton to Dorchester, opened in 1847 and running via Ringwood, Wimborne and Broadstone.

On 9 April 1967, just three months before the end of Southern steam workings, the LCGB ran the 'Hampshire Branch Lines Rail Tour'. This visited various lines in Hampshire and Dorset, including the Lymington branch. The train was hauled to Lymington by BR Class 4 2-6-4T No 80151 with Ivatt Class 2 2-6-2T No 41320 at the rear. On the return leg from Lymington, and with No 41320 now leading, the special draws near to the junction with the main line. The Lymington branch was also included in the conversion to third-rail electrical traction, and the conductor rail is seen already in place.

Right: Another LCGB special visited the Lymington branch just over a year earlier, on 19 March 1966. With the daylight fading fast, enthusiasts take some final pictures as the setting sun highlights the unconventional form of Bulleid Class Q 0-6-0 No 33006 alongside the estuary next to the signalbox at Lymington Pier. No 33006, built by the Southern Railway in 1942, had been officially withdrawn from service in January 1966, two months before the date of this railtour!

Right: Back on the main line near Sway, and with the shadows beginning to lengthen, BR Class 5 4-6-0 No 73169 sweeps by with a train which Norman Lockett recorded as a Bournemouth to Eastleigh service. This, the present-day direct line from Brockenhurst to Bournemouth, via Sway to Christchurch, was opened in 1888. Christchurch had already been linked to the original main line to Dorchester by means of a branch line from Ringwood, opened in 1862, which, in turn, was extended to Bournemouth East in 1870.

Left: With the end of Southern Region steam less than a year away, the external condition of BR Class 4 2-6-0 No 76029 reflects the lack of attention then prevalent as it pulls away from the east end of Bournemouth Central with an up train. The Bedford Dormobile and Ford Anglia in the background appear better cared for! Only recently, after many decades of neglect and at least one threat of demolition, has the station's overall roof been restored and re-glazed.

Below: The view of the locomotive depot at Bournemouth (former shed code 71B) as seen from the station down platform. A variety of Bulleid and BR 'Standard' motive power is on view. Rebuilt 'West Country' light Pacific No 34101 *Hartland* is prepared for a next turn of duty. Also visible are a BR Class 4 2-6-4T and unmodified 'WC' 4-6-2 No 34041 *Wilton*, a Bournemouth engine of long standing which, until a few years previously, had seen service over the Somerset & Dorset line.

Above: Two studies of sunshine and shadows... With the safety valves erupting, 'Battle of Britain' class 4-6-2 No 34076 *41 Squadron* prepares to leave Bournemouth Central with a train for Waterloo, having taken over the service from a 'Merchant Navy' which had brought the train in from Weymouth.

Right: The doyen of the Bulleid light Pacifics, rebuilt 'West Country' class No 34001 *Exeter* pulls away from the down platform at Bournemouth Central on the last leg of a journey from Waterloo to Bournemouth West. The signalbox at Bournemouth can be seen in its elevated position above the station platform. The building on the left is the motive power depot. The elevated signalbox can be seen above the platform canopy.

Above: With a lightweight load, 'Merchant Navy' Pacific No 35016 *Elders Fyffes* passes through the attractive cutting on the approach towards the western end of Bournemouth Central. The siding to the right was the longer of two lines to the west of Central station used for berthing empty stock. The species of tree bordering both sides of the railway is that which gave the 'Pines Express' its title!

Right: A little over a mile farther west from the previous view finds another attractive lineside location. 'Merchant Navy' class No 35028 *Clan Line* leads the 'Bournemouth Belle' through a cutting near Talbot Woods on the approach to Gasworks Junction, where the train veered left for the final mile to the terminus at Bournemouth West. (The distance from Bournemouth Central to Bournemouth West by rail was about 3½ miles, whereas, measured in a direct line, the two stations were less than half this distance apart!) *Clan Line* was the first of its class to be purchased for preservation and restored to working order, and has since made countless main-line trips.

Above: Bournemouth West appears to have held a special appeal for Norman Lockett, and some difficulty has been experienced in selecting just a few pictures from the large choice available! This opening shot provides a panorama of the station, with 'Battle of Britain' class No 34061 *73 Squadron* having just backed down onto its stock in Platform 1 whilst BR Class 5 4-6-0 No 73117 waits to leave with a train for Waterloo. The tall brick building in the centre distance is the Midland Hotel — just about the only part of this scene recognisable today!

Right: Looking northwestwards from the platform end, 'Battle of Britain' No 34066 *Spitfire* approaches the terminus at the end of a run from Waterloo, passing the station pilot, a Drummond Class M7 0-4-4T, No 30036. This view shows how the gradient rose (initially at 1 in 90) right from the platform end, passing the Bournemouth West signalbox (seen in the mid-distance) towards the junction of the lines to Branksome and Bournemouth Central, controlled by another signalbox at Bournemouth West Junction.

Left: The first of a trio of pictures featuring the 'Bournemouth Belle'. 'Merchant Navy' Pacific No 35026 *Lamport & Holt Line* awaits departure from Platform 4 at 4.30pm. Notice that the leading vehicle is a standard BR carriage in chocolate and cream livery — the nearest match to the Pullman livery of this famous train!

Right: Portrait of a top-link driver. Can any reader name the driver of No 35026?

Below right: Providing a welcome push at the rear, a BR Class 4 2-6-4T assists departure from the station. A passenger in Pullman Car No 63 appears to have spotted the photographer. Just look at the condition of those Pullman coaches — what a marvellous way to travel, and all for a supplementary fee (in the late 1950s) of 6 shillings (30 pence) First-class and 4s (20p) Second-class, all the way to Waterloo!

'Battle of Britain' No 34064 *Fighter Command*, the Bulleid Pacific only recently fitted with an oblong Giesl ejector, is entrusted with the 'Bournemouth Belle'. Whether this was in conjunction with any road-testing of the modified Pacific is not known. The ejector was installed in an attempt to counteract the loss of efficiency normally associated with the use of a spark-arrester; the latter having been fitted to No 34064 as an experiment to reduce the propensity of the unmodified Pacifics to set fire to the lineside! The locomotive was withdrawn from service in May 1966, just 20 months after being photographed here by Norman Lockett. The 'Bournemouth Belle' lasted only a little longer, the final train running (from Bournemouth Central, the West station having already closed) on Sunday 9 July 1967.

A Bulleid Pacific which suffered a much kinder fate, modified 'West Country' No 34027 *Taw Valley* awaits the road to run light-engine to the motive power depot at Bournemouth Central, having arrived earlier with the 10am service from Brighton. Note the slight damage to the running plate above the cylinder casing. *Taw Valley* was withdrawn in August 1964, but was later purchased for preservation and beautifully restored to main-line-running condition.

Above: One of Norman Lockett's earliest colour views at Bournemouth West dates from Sunday 7 September 1958. Basking in the sunshine, 'Lord Nelson' class 4-6-0 No 30862 *Lord Collingwood* waits to leave with the 1.8pm (Sundays) train to Southampton. No 30862, which entered service in 1929, was withdrawn in October 1962.

Right: Possibly the finest shot by Norman Lockett featuring the 'Bournemouth Belle' at Bournemouth West. In a condition that befitted this famous train, 'Merchant Navy' class No 35030 *Elder Dempster Lines* prepares for a prompt departure.

Below: On the western side of Bournemouth, the routes from the Central and West stations came together at Branksome, so forming a triangle of lines. Beyond Branksome, BR Class 4 2-6-0 No 76056 drifts down the grade with a stopping train to Weymouth, having just passed under the attractive three-arch overbridge spanning the cutting near the summit of Parkstone Bank, which carried the line down to sea level on the approach to Poole.

Right: Climbing a 1-in-60 section of the bank between Parkstone and Branksome stations, Drummond Class M7 0-4-4T No 30111 propels two coaches forming the 12.8pm 'push and pull' train from Brockenhurst, via Ringwood and Broadstone, to Bournemouth. Ivo Peters was also at the lineside and recorded that the locomotive 'was wheezing somewhat'! By the start of the following summer (1964), all of the remaining 'M7' 0-4-4Ts, so long a feature on these push-and-pull trains centred on Bournemouth and surrounding areas, would be but a thing of the past.

Contrasts at Hamworthy Junction. Beyond Poole, the main line to Weymouth crosses Holes Bay to reach Hamworthy Junction. Bathed in late-winter sunshine, BR Class 9F 2-10-0 No 92209 reverses through the station whilst running round a special train — the 'South Western Rambler' — organised by the Southern Counties Touring Society on 8 March 1964. The 2-10-0 had arrived via the original line to Hamworthy Junction, which ran direct from Broadstone.

In contrast, on a very wet day ex-LNER Gresley 'A3' Pacific No 60112 *St Simon* had brought in another special run by the SCTS on 25 August 1963. Before continuing the tour to Weymouth, the 'A3' waits at Hamworthy Junction whilst the special makes a return run along the freight-only branch to Lower Hamworthy behind 'M7' class 0-4-4T No 30052.

Left: The short branch line running south from Hamworthy Junction was the first railway to serve the town of Poole, reached by means of the toll bridge which spanned the waters linking Holes Bay and Poole Harbour. The original Poole station, built at Lower Hamworthy, closed to passengers as long ago as 1893, but the branch remains open to this day as a freight-only line. In 1963 Norman Lockett photographed *Western Pride*, one of a pair of 0-4-0 saddle tanks acquired by Southern Wharves Ltd to shunt its complex of private sidings at Hamworthy Wharf. *Western Pride* was built by Robert Stephenson & Hawthorn Ltd in 1949 (Works No 7545) and was numbered by its owner as 2. A sister engine, No 1 *Bonnie Prince Charlie*,

was later preserved by the Great Western Society at Didcot; No 2, however, went for scrap.

Above: Wareham was the junction for the Swanage branch, although the branch proper left the main line at Worgret Junction, a mile to the west. BR Class 4 2-6-4T No 80066 calls at Wareham with a Weymouth to Bournemouth stopping train. These fine locomotives were introduced in 1951, the example here being constructed at Brighton and entering traffic the following year. Several have been restored, including two by the Southern Steam Trust which are normally based at Swanage.

Left: For more than 30 years, the Drummond Class M7 0-4-4 tanks were the mainstay of everyday branch trains serving the line to Swanage. Against the backdrop of East Hill, No 30379 climbs away from Corfe Castle and towards Eldon's Siding with a Swanage to Wareham train. Thankfully, and against all odds, this scene has now been re-created on the magnificently-restored Swanage Railway.

One of the many specials which traversed the Swanage branch towards the end of the steam era, this tour was organised by the LCGB and ran on 27 February 1967. Viewed from the slopes below Corfe Castle, a pair of Ivatt 2-6-2 tanks, Nos 41284 and 41301, drift down the grade and are about to pass over Corfe Viaduct. This section of the line across the viaduct was taken up in 1972. Twenty years later it was relaid, but with a financial crisis then threatening the very future of the Swanage Railway, the line from Harman's Cross to the present operational railhead (the very successful 'Park & Ride' station at Norden, just a little to the left of this view) was not 'reopened' to traffic until August 1995.

Above: With Corfe Castle as the backdrop, an LCGB 'Dorset Coast Express' heads across Corfe Common towards Afflington on Sunday 7 May 1967. The special is headed by 'West Country' class No 34023 *Blackmore Vale* (now preserved and based on the Bluebell Railway), with BR Class 4 2-6-4T No 80011 on the rear of the train — an operating necessity, as, by this date, insufficient facilities remained at Swanage to release the Bulleid Pacific from the front of the train. Today, of course, it is once again possible to travel across Corfe Common behind either a Bulleid Pacific or a BR Class 4 tank.

Right: Viewed from the Victoria Road overbridge, BR Class 4 2-6-0 No 76010 gathers speed and heads up the gradient away from Swanage during the final summer of steam-hauled services over the branch. Looking into the middle distance, have the exertions of No 76010 just set fire to the lineside? This was the first section of the branch to be restored to passenger traffic by the Swanage Railway, with public services as far as Herston, on the outskirts of Swanage, commencing on Good Friday 1984.

Another view of the 'Dorset Coast Express', following arrival at Swanage. BR Class 4 2-6-4T No 80011 waits to head the train back to Wareham, with No 34023 *Blackmore Vale* now trailing at the rear. Swanage signalbox, closed in June 1967, was demolished towards the end of that same year. As this caption is written, a superb new signalbox (built in the same LSWR style, but larger in size) is nearing completion on the opposite side of the line, and, soon, signalling will again form a part of the scene at this delightful terminus.

No 76010, waiting to leave Swanage, was destined to work the final steam-hauled passenger service from the station just a few weeks later, on 4 September 1966. Having lost its tracks, and part of the platform, following closure at the start of 1972, now, almost 30 years later, the station looks remarkably similar to this scene — a tribute to all those associated with the Swanage Railway Project. The backdrop has changed, however: the brick-built hotel to the left succumbed to redevelopment, whilst, more recently, much of the site of the former station yard has become a supermarket.

Left: A visitor on tour to the Southern Region. On 4 June 1967, the (then) recently-restored ex-LNER Class A4 Pacific No 4498 *Sir Nigel Gresley* makes a vigorous climb towards Moreton, about 5 miles east of Dorchester, with a special train from Waterloo to Weymouth. This was the second of two railtours, made on consecutive days, which had been organised by the A4 Locomotive Society Ltd.

Right: Just three days before the final Southern Region steam workings, rebuilt 'Battle of Britain' class No 34060 *25 Squadron* emerges from the gloom of the 814yd-long Bincombe Tunnel, 3 miles south of Dorchester, and heads down the steep gradient towards Weymouth with a train from Bournemouth. The smokebox numberplate, together with nameplate and associated plaque bearing the coat of arms of 25 Squadron, had already been removed.

Below: Unmodified 'Battle of Britain' No 34086 *219 Squadron* drifts down the 1-in-52 bank with the 10.12am (Sundays) service from Bournemouth to Weymouth. The tunnel seen in this and the previous view is the longer of two at Bincombe. No 34086 is about to enter the much shorter tunnel which lies immediately to the north of the site of the former Upwey Wishing Well Halt.

Below: Rebuilt 'West Country' No 34037 *Clovelly,* with a Waterloo to Weymouth express, passes through Radipole Halt, the final station before reaching the terminus at Weymouth. Just a few days later, with the end of Southern Region steam workings and only nine years after rebuilding, No 34037 would be withdrawn and stored awaiting disposal to Messrs Cashmore's yard at Newport for cutting-up.

Leaving Weymouth with a train for Bournemouth, BR Class 4 2-6-0 No 76005 commences the climb out of Weymouth with a lightweight load comprising two coaches still in the Southern Region green livery and a rear coach in the then-new corporate BR image which (sadly) lasted far too long! The two tracks in the foreground gave access to the motive power depot at Weymouth.

On a Sunday in early May 1961, 'Lord Nelson' class 4-6-0 No 30858 *Lord Duncan* rests between turns at the side of the locomotive shed at Weymouth MPD. A Maunsell design dating from 1926, No 30858 displays the large-diameter chimney — one of several modifications made by Bulleid from 1938.

They still turned locomotives the hard way at Weymouth! With steam erupting from the safety valves and the blower on, 'Battle of Britain' class No 34086 *219 Squadron* is turned on the 60ft-diameter table prior to making a return working to Bournemouth. I wonder if some previous derailment (or worse!) had influenced the placing of the notice warning 'ALL ENGINES must STOP before going on this TURNTABLE' ?

A train of containers holding perishables traffic, unloaded from a Channel Islands steam ferry, is slowly hauled along the quayside by 0-6-0PT No 7780. Note the bell behind the toolbox on the running board. On this occasion the quay appears to be reasonably free of cars, but delays to rail traffic (particularly during the holiday season) were inevitably the result of drivers' parking their vehicles foul of the railway.

Above: The fascination of steam! A small boy and, no doubt, his father watch 0-6-0PT No 3737 engaged in marshalling a train of vans at the Quay station. I wonder how many generations of boys, on seeing a plume of steam at the quayside, persuaded an elder to forsake the beach temporarily to view a train passing through the streets along the tramway at Weymouth? The building in the background is the Weymouth Pavilion Theatre and, judging by the notice above the central entrance doors, Tommy Trinder was 'top of the bill' for the early-summer season in 1961.

Above right: It's not only the green-coloured coaching stock which provides a reminder that the Southern Region was in full operating control at Weymouth Quay by the end of the 1950s. A new ship — the *Caesarea*, seen here — was provided for the SR in 1961 for the Channel Islands boat traffic.

Right: This final view is of the branch line which, until closure in 1965, ran from the main line at Weymouth to the Isle of Portland. Passenger trains had ceased as long ago as 1952. An SCTS special in Southern Region livery crosses the Fleet Viaduct on the run to Portland, 'topped and tailed' by ex-GW pannier tanks 4689 and 7782 — a rather appropriate combination of stock and motive power for a line which had once been owned jointly by the LSWR and the GWR.

Index of Locations illustrated

Bincombe	71, 72
Bournemouth Central	44, 45, 46, 47, 48
Bournemouth (Talbot Woods)	49
Bournemouth West	50, 51, 52, 53, 54, 55, 56, 57
Branksome (near)	58, 59
Brockenhurst	40, 41
Corfe Castle	64, 65, 66
Eastleigh MPD	16, 17, 18, 19
Fareham	15
Hamworthy Junction	60, 61
Hamworthy Wharf	62
Havant	4, 5, 6, 11, 12, 13
Hayling Island	8
Langstone (near)	7, 9, 10
Lymington Junction (near)	42
Lymington Pier	43
Millbrook	38
Moreton (near)	70
Portsmouth Harbour	20
Radipole	73
Ryde Esplanade	22, 23
Ryde Pier Head	Front cover, 21
Ryde St John's Road	24, 25, 26, 27
Shanklin	30
Smallbrook Junction	28, 29
Southampton Central	1, 32, 33, 34, 35, 36
Southampton Docks	37
Swanage	67, 68, 69
Sway (near)	43
Totton	39
Ventnor	31
Wareham	63
Weymouth	74, 75, 76
Weymouth (Portland branch)	79
Weymouth Quay	Back cover, 77, 78, 79
Wickham	14

Front cover: Ryde Pier Head station, the railway 'gateway' to the Isle of Wight. It's a glorious summer day in 1964 and the South Coast mainland is clearly visible in the right background. Two of the island's Class O2 0-4-4T locomotives, No 18 *Ningwood* (nearer, at Platform 2) and No 14 *Fishbourne* (standing at Platform 1) await departure with trains for Cowes and Ventnor respectively.

Back cover: Weymouth Quay. Ex-GWR 0-6-0 pannier tank No 1368 runs light-engine along the quay, passing the Royal Oak Inn and heading towards the junction with the main line. This scene dates from early May 1961. Note the warning bell carried on the running plate — a requirement for all locomotives working over the quayside lines.

Acknowledgements

Where it has been necessary to seek or confirm information contained in the captions in this book, particular use has been made of the Ivo Peters Collection, courtesy Julian Peters, and of the *Railway Magazine*, together, to a lesser extent, with other journals and publications too numerous to list individually.